Backyard Chickens for Beginners: Getting the Best Chickens, Choosing Coops, Feeding and Care, and Beating City Chicken Laws

By R.J. Ruppenthal, Attorney/Professor/Garden Writer

- Fresh Eggs Every Day
- How Much Space Do You Need?
- Building or Buying a Coop
- Feeders, Waterers, Nesting Boxes, and Roosts
- Getting Chicks or Chickens
- Feeding Your Chickens
- Tips for Cold Climates
- Health and Safety
- Dealing with Neighbors, City Chicken Laws, and Other Challenges
- Resources: Everything You Need!

Chapter 1: Fresh Eggs Every Day

How would you like to enjoy fresh eggs every day? Even in small urban homes, most backyards can support 3-4 egg-laying hens, either ranging freely or in an enclosed run area. Hens in their prime lay an egg almost every day. Three hens will give you at least a dozen fresh eggs every week, and probably more. With four hens, you can almost guarantee two dozen eggs per week…no roosters needed.

On top of that, chickens are entertaining pets, they are great around kids, and they help you reduce your impact on the environment. This booklet will take you through everything you need to know before starting your own home chicken flock.

Chickens are the easiest pets you will ever have. They can eat your kitchen scraps and clean your yard of bugs, reducing the cost of commercial feed to a few bucks a month. Your time commitment will be 5-10 minutes per day to check on them, feed them, and change their water every few days.

About once a month, you also need to spend a couple of hours cleaning their coop area, shoveling out old bedding and manure into your compost bin or compost tumbler, then replacing it with some sawdust, straw, or shredded paper. That's about it! Keeping chickens is pretty simple.

To get started with chickens, you need to know the basics of how to buy or build a coop, the proper space requirements for your coop and run area, and a few additional items you will need such as feeders and waterers (all are available for only a few dollars at local farm stores, pet stores, or online). In this booklet, you also will learn how to obtain chickens, either from hatching eggs, newborn chicks, or teenage pullets ready to lay. And we will cover essential information on how and what to feed your chickens, cold climate tips, and keeping chickens safe and healthy.

A booklet on city chickens would not be complete without addressing some challenges that arise in urban areas: small space restrictions, lousy neighbors, zoning ordinances, and questions about noise levels and smells. No obstacle should prevent you from raising a few egg-laying hens, but I want to arm you with the right information to win any battle.

Finally, you get a Resources section that is worth the price of this booklet all by itself. It directs you to more information (which you *do not* have to pay for) on learning about chicken breeds, finding chickens, chicken coops and supplies, getting your questions answered, and more. Some other "how to" books add filler pages to cover this extra material and they charge you for it. But if the same information is available for free online, why pay for it? Stick with this booklet for the basic info you need, and I will show you the rest of it online *for free*.

Once you finish reading this booklet, you will have all the knowledge you need to get started with chickens, plus you will have online access to all resources and support you may need. Get ready for a homegrown omelet with the best and most nutritious organic eggs you have ever tasted!

Chapter 2: How Much Space Do You Need?

The term "chicken coop" has different meanings to different people. In this booklet, the "coop" is the structure where chickens go to spend the night. In addition to this coop, they will have some kind of outdoor run area, whether this is free range or enclosed. Some people mix these two areas together and call them both a "coop". To keep things clear, I will refer to the inside area as the "coop" and the outside area as the "run".

Happy chickens lay lots of eggs, so it is in your basic self-interest to keep them happy. Happy chickens need a minimum of four (4) square feet of coop space per bird, plus a run area of at least ten (10) square feet per bird. I base these numbers on the recommendations of Gail Damerow in *Storey's Guide to Raising Chickens* (Storey Publishing 2010, see Resources section).

If there is no outside run area, then chickens need ten (10) square feet of coop space per bird. I will ignore this last suggestion, because you should not be keeping chickens if you cannot provide them with some outside space to move around in (whether this space is free range or in an enclosed pen). So let's look at the first number: four (4) square feet of coop space per bird.

If your chickens are outside most of the time, basically using the coop just for sleeping and laying eggs, then four (4) square feet per bird is adequate. If chickens are kept in the coop for long periods when they cannot go outside, especially if you are trying to overwinter them inside, then they need extra coop space. The proper coop size also depends on the size of the chickens you are keeping. Bantams are much smaller than standard birds, so you can fit more of them in any given coop.

Even for standard birds, there is a big difference between an eight pound Orpington and a five pound Ameracauna hen. For medium-sized breeds like Ameracauna, I would feel more comfortable using the minimum size, while a flock of larger birds like Orpys could get pretty crowded with only four (4) square feet per bird. Tight conditions make for more fighting and risk of disease, so give them plenty of space.

Let's apply the four (4) square foot recommendation in the small backyard setting. *Two hens* would need a coop of at least eight (8) square feet, say two feet by four feet (2' x 4'). *Three hens* would need twelve (12) square feet, which might be a three by four foot (3' x 4') coop. *Four hens* would need sixteen (16) square feet, which could be accomplished with either a four by four (4' x 4') square coop or a more rectangular three and a half by five (3.5' x 5'). This should not seem like a lot of space, since it is only a few inches larger than a standard-sized bathtub.

But the outdoor run area will take up the most space. The run area should provide at least ten (10) square feet of space for each chicken. Again, this is a minimum, which I would increase by a few feet if the feeder and waterer take up part of the space. So let's crack the numbers again to see how this looks for a city dweller with a small backyard. *Two hens* would need a run space of at least twenty (20) square feet, perhaps three and a half feet by six feet (3.5' x 6'). *Three hens* would need thirty (30) square feet, either in a block of around five by six feet (5' x 6') or a strip such as three by ten feet (3' x 10'). *Four hens* would need forty (40) square feet, which you could create with a five by eight foot (5' x 8') block or a four by ten foot (4' x 10') plot.

Do not ignore side yards as possible run areas. At my daughter's former school, which has two hens we donated, they keep the chickens in a coop attached to a long, narrow fenced strip next to the building. This pen, which the children can walk inside to play with the chickens and harvest eggs, is only about three feet wide, but at least 20 feet long. It could have been used as a long flower bed at one time.

At only three feet wide, I may never have seriously considered this for a chicken area, but it provides these two hens with plenty of run space. There are some shelves and an old rabbit hutch on one end, which were turned into an open-sided coop. The coop is covered from the rain and the climate is quite mild, so the chickens do not complain that it is only enclosed on only three sides. Their wild ancestors slept in trees, not small houses.

The run space does not need to be square or rectangular, though that is usually the easiest way to go. In the run area, make sure to have some perches they can roost on during the day; I use one-inch thick dowels or garden stakes, placed 2-3 feet off the ground. The main concern with the run is to keep it covered with plenty of mulch or bedding. Chicken manure makes the soil toxic very quickly, but this can be balanced (and odors nearly eliminated) with the addition of some carbon-rich mulch/bedding.

A thick layer of straw, leaves, shredded paper, or sawdust as bedding will help the chicken manure decompose naturally and create a balanced compost. Keep at least a few inches of this mulch on the ground at all times, and change it every couple of months. Old chicken bedding with manure can go right into a compost bin or tumbler, where it will decompose and make a rich addition to your garden soil the next year.

My chickens have a fully enclosed run which is a little larger than this minimum size. I built this enclosure with a frame of 1 ½ x 1 ½ inch wooden stakes, covered with half inch wire mesh that is secured by large staples. Part of the run is shaded by the coop, which sits on top of it, providing some protection from the elements on hot or rainy days. Even the bottom of the run is lined with poultry wire, though the soil and mulch on top of it are deep enough that the chickens never scratch down to the wire.

The coop is open to the run, so that the chickens can use it every day. If I am away from home, this is where they spend the day. I do not need to close anything up at night because the coop and run are sealed. Predators and pests (such as raccoons and rats) cannot get in.

When I am home, there is a gate I can open to give them more outdoor space. Attached to the gate is an extended run area behind my raised vegetable beds and under some fruit trees. It is lined with temporary plastic fences to keep the chickens out of my vegetable garden, and since I do not consider these fences very strong, I only let the chickens out into this area when I am home (which may only be an hour or two in the morning or evening).

These fences, in turn, are attached to a third run area, which is made from a couple of temporary dog fences. I move this around, sometimes letting them into part of the yard to eat weeds and bugs, and other times directing them onto one of my raised beds, which they can scratch in for a few months at a time. They aerate and fertilize the soil, which I often cover with compost or mulch that they dig in for me. Here is a picture of them doing their thing in part of a raised bed, which has a movable, temporary fence protecting the vegetables and blueberries.

The chickens love to take dust baths in this deep soil also, which is an important part of their hygiene and pest protection. A months or two after letting them into the bed, they will have it thoroughly transformed (though I cannot plant in the soil until their manure breaks down a bit, say 6-12 months, since the ammonia needs to convert to plant-usable nitrogen). After a hawk dropped in one day and tried to attack a full-sized hen, I covered the extended run with plastic bird netting. Putting this on only took a few minutes because it does not need to be secured too well; the mere sight of it seems to keep chickens in and hawks out.

Chapter 3: Building or Buying a Coop

What do a Swiss chalet, vintage car body, converted storage cabinet, and miniature trailer on wheels have in common? These are just a few of the many thousands of coop designs people use. Whether you choose to buy a coop or build your own, you will find a nearly endless array of designs available. Some of the craftspeople who specialize in making chicken coops are truly gifted people who make gorgeous and long-lasting structures.

Hand-crafted coops can be quite expensive, while on the opposite extreme, you can build one yourself out of scavenged materials that do not cost a dime. Your main concerns should be that this coop meets the chickens' needs, keeps out predators and pests, can be cleaned easily, lasts long enough to make the buying or building of it worthwhile, and has enough visual appeal to be accepted into your yard. Each of these concerns is covered below.

Building a Coop

When I put my coop together, there were very few coop plans available. I found some free plans on the Internet, and people were selling others on eBay. Today, there is *much* more free material out there. The Backyard Chicken website (www.backyardchickens.com, click on "Coops") provides free plans for more than 1,000 user-submitted coop designs. The people who run this site provide a wonderful service to the community.

Buying a coop can be expensive, and you may not save too much if you build your own from premium materials. But if you can find ways to economize or scavenge some materials, you could make a good coop for almost no cost. For example, if you or a neighbor is building a fence or remodeling a house, you might get some old wood or surplus new wood for no added cost.

There is no rule requiring you to build a coop from wood, either, if you find the right bargain on some metal, plastic, or composite material. I have even seen coops built from stone. You also may be able to economize on roofing materials if you choose to cover your coop this way. It costs money to buy your own materials, but if someone is getting a house re-roofed, you might get a few extra feet of tar paper and some spare shingles at no extra charge.

If you are building with wood (as most people will), then use thick pieces, not flimsy siding. A nicely built coop can last for many years. Thinner and lighter wood can warp and split where it is joined by screws or nails. This creates opportunities for predators and pests. Unless you are using a truly rot-resistant wood, make sure you paint or stain the surfaces to preserve it. Many eco-friendly options are available these days. It is a good idea to use more than one coat. You could use pressure treated wood as an alternative, but it can contain some very toxic copper and arsenic.

Speaking of screws and nails, screws tend to be the longer-lasting choice. They will hold wood together tightly and allow less warping than nails, plus you always can tighten them again later (or unscrew them if you need to disassemble and make repairs). Since I live in a moist climate, I used vinyl-coated screws on my coop. I know some hardcore environmentalists do not like vinyl, but I don't think my chickens will be eating many screws.

If you still have some small gaps in the coop despite your best efforts, one thing you can do is to cover the gaps with poultry wire and staple it in. As with any use of wire near chickens, make sure sharp edges are turned down. You do not want anything to hurt your chickens.

Before building a coop, also read the material on Chickens' Needs and Keeping Out Predators and Pests (below, in this same chapter).

Buying a Coop

Buying a coop can be as simple as going down to your local hardware store and putting down a credit card. Or it may be as simple as searching for coops online and clicking a few buttons. Since the urban gardening and backyard chicken movements have expanded in recent years, so too have the coops. My local pet store did not used to sell coops, but now they do. During this same time, the hardware store has added compost bins and raised beds, so I think coops are only a matter of time.

Coops will soon be standard backyard "appliances" in many urban yards as chickens become some of the most common pets. It just makes a lot more sense to grow your own protein than to subsidize factory farms that keep their birds in cramped conditions, feed them imbalanced food, dope them up with hormones and antibiotics, and then add to the price and carbon impact by shipping them through the supermarket chain of distribution.

Though it is simple to buy a coop, you must be sure you get the right one to fit your needs. It should be big enough for your chickens, well made, appropriate for your space, and close to your intended budget. I would hesitate to buy a coop on the Internet, sight unseen. If it has to be shipped any significant distance, this can really increase the overall cost also. If they offer free shipping to send it long distances to you, then that just means the shipping cost has been included in the overall price. On the other hand, there are so many more choices online than you may find locally. My advice is to look locally first, and then if you cannot find what you want, order one online.

There are several reasons to buy local. First, you will not incur unreasonable shipping costs. Some local craftspeople may charge a small delivery fee, but this is a lot less than you would pay to ship a coop across the country. Second, beware that there are scam artists out there who will take your money up front and provide nothing. Any local craftsperson should let you examine the merchandise first, which will also allow you to check the quality of construction.

By perusing local classified ads, you may even find a used coop that someone is giving away or selling for very little. Browse through local classified ads such as those on your regional Craigslist (www.craigslist.org), which has a "For Sale" category with a "Farm+Garden" link. I have seen some good used coops on this site before, but at the time I did not have quick access to a truck with which to pick them up. If you have a farm store or feed store in your area that sells poultry supplies, ask if they can refer you to a good local coop maker.

If you must buy online and have it shipped to you, then start with a Google or Yahoo search. What you will find quickly is that well made coops often start around $400-$600 and this might not even include shipping. The really cute coops often cost twice that much. Good materials and labor are expensive these days. Some craftspeople make a cottage industry of this and if they can sell coops at that price, then who can blame them for charging what they can?

Bear in mind that a well-made coop can last for many years, and a lesser quality one may need to be replaced during that time, so it may be a worthwhile investment up front. To see a few examples (which I do not endorse but seem to be well-made) try www.comfycoops.com, www.winecountrycoops.com, and www.greenchickencoop.com. This site sells some reasonably priced coops that are not quite as fancy. www.coopsnmore.com.

By searching large online retailer sites like Amazon, Petco, and Sears, you will notice that there are some prefabricated coops on the low end of the price scale. Many of these are made by a company called Ware. I have not used any Ware products before. But I know people who have Ware coops and I have read enough online reviews of prefabs to form a secondhand opinion of their quality. In general, prefabs make serviceable starter coops, but usually these are built using the cheapest available materials. Some users have reported that the wood will be cracked when they open up the box or that the door locks fall off within a few weeks (and do not protect well against predator intrusions anyway).

If you are prepared to start replacing things and strengthening the coop almost immediately, then a prefabricated coop might last awhile and save you some money over the more expensive options. At least it provides something to start with and a structure that you can build on as needed. But if you are looking for a coop that does not need this high level of maintenance, then be prepared to spend more money up front for something really well made. Some of the mobile coops described below may be affordable options as well.

Another idea is to find someone in your area who is handy at making things, print out some online plans for a coop you like, and offer to buy this person any needed materials as well as pay a reasonable price for labor. Maybe the woodshop teacher at your local high school has a star pupil or a local cabinetmaker has an apprentice who will moonlight on a weekend. Or perhaps you have a friend or family member who will make the coop in exchange for free pizza.

Chicken Tractors and Mobile Coops

Whoever first had this idea is a genius, because mobile chicken coops are a perfect idea in small yards. The coop and a small run are put on wheels so they can be pulled like a cart or dolly from one part of the property to another. While the run space is not that large (after all, you have to lug it), chicken tractors can be moved as often as you like, giving the chickens a new area of ground with each move. They can eat the bugs and some new grass each time. As the chicken tractor is moved around your yard, eventually the birds will fertilize different spots and improve the health of your soil and lawn (make sure you use no pesticides on the lawn). You can see some great pictures of different Chicken Tractors on the City Chicken site (http://thecitychicken.com). And here is a picture of one; notice that it is too difficult to pick up and carry, but is one wheels so it may be moved like a wheelbarrow.

There are some great do-it-yourself plans for building chicken tractors online. Start with the Backyard Chickens subcategory for chicken tractor designs (http://www.backyardchickens.com) . Of course, you can buy a chicken tractor as well. Try running an online Google or Yahoo search for "chicken tractor" or "mobile chicken coop" to find some. Another design that is frequently sold online is a "chicken ark", which is a small A-frame coop that sits on top of a triangular run area. It often has poles extending on each end of the base so that two people can move it around a yard, making the ark another option for mobile cooping.

No discussion of movable coops would be complete without mentioning the Eglu. The Eglu is a British product which is also sold internationally; the U.S. site is located at http://www.omlet.us. People either love or hate the Eglu design; it looks like a cross between a chicken coop and an iPod. The plastic construction reportedly makes it easy to clean, while the attached run area is a nice addition. It is quite portable, which is good, since the run does not offer that much space for chickens.

Or you can do what I do, which is to have a permanent, stationary chicken coop, plus an added run that changes. I use portable dog fences for the changing run area and just connect it to the coop and permanent run by means of a gate or poultry wire tunnel. Since I have raised beds, and I do not want the hens scratching up my veggie garden, I let them into one raised bed at a time which they can de-bug and fertilize, before moving them to another raised bed or other section of the yard.

The Chickens' Needs

The coop offers chickens a place to spend the night. Inside the coop, they will stay drier and warmer than they would outside. You can attach a nesting box or two to the coop also, and they will return to the coop to lay eggs each day. But contrary to popular belief, chickens do not curl up at night in a warm nest of straw or feathers. The nesting box is where they lay eggs, but not where they prefer to sleep.

Chickens sleep while they are perched on something they can curl their toes around. Installing one-inch thick dowels, sticks, or small branches across the inside of the coop allows chickens to mimic their wild ancestors, who slept in trees at night. Their perches should be set as high up as possible in the coop, but far enough from the nesting boxes that they do not poop near them.

Keeping Out Predators and Pests

Most predators hunt at nighttime. Even urban areas have their fair share. Raccoons are probably the cleverest, most prolific large mammals, and they thrive in all but the densest city neighborhoods. Opossums, foxes, coyotes, bobcats, skunks, badgers, weasels, and ferrets are additional predators that may exist in your region. Rats are more of a pest, but they can attack chickens at night also. An additional problem in cities can be posed by neighborhood dogs; whoever said that "good fences make good neighbors" certainly had it right.

It is important to know what predators you may be up against. It is one thing to make a coop raccoon-proof, but if you live in bear country this may not be enough. It you have problems with rats or anything in the weasel family, these animals can squeeze through impossibly small spaces. You may not even know there is a space between two boards on your coop until one of these creatures finds in and you learn the hard way by losing some hens.

There are two keys to predator-proofing your coop: strong construction and no gaps. Strong construction means the coop should be built of thick materials that are not easily torn off or chewed through by a determined animal. If you buy a prefabricated coop that appears to be pretty flimsy, you may need to improve upon it. For example, you could cover weak parts with another layer of scrap wood. Paint the whole thing nicely if you are worried about aesthetics. Give the coop a quick visual inspection every few days, because an animal who starts chewing a hole may continue the job another night.

Gaps can be tough to spot, but you need to become good at finding them before predators and rodents do. Examine any places where boards come together or where wire from a run is joining the coop. If you see even a half inch gap, tighten it up with some extra screws. Wherever wire joins wood, use heavy duty staples at frequent intervals; raccoons can pull out lesser staples.

Make sure nothing can dig in underneath the coop or run. I leave one door in my chickens' coop that I can open and close to clean it, and this is tightly secured by its locks. Two small exterior windows are protected with poultry wire, which is stapled inside the coop. The only open door to the coop faces into the primary run area, which is tightly enclosed by poultry wire with half-inch mesh.

Rats got into my run before I realized that I had left a small gap near the ground. Once I sealed it, they disappeared. I stopped their tunneling underneath by hammering in 6-inch tall plastic landscape edging around all sides of the run (I hammered it all the way in). After much tweaking and tightening, I think the only creatures that could find their way into my coop and run now would be the smallest of mice, and I have not noticed any sign of them.

Easy to Clean Coops

The main work of cleaning a coop involves scooping out all the old bedding and manure, which I do once a month. You can use any carbon-rich mulch material as bedding, including leaves, straw, sawdust, or shredded paper. If you use a thick bedding layer at the bottom of the coop, and cover fresh poop with a handful of bedding material every few days, the coop will not produce many odors. Having some vents or an open window screened with predator wire (weather permitting) also helps with odor control.

The other necessary function is having a wide door that you can open to scoop out the waste material. I have seen a few coops with a bottom that slides out for waste disposal, but scooping it out does not take too long either. When you open the door to clean out the coop, you need to be sure that no perches or wire mesh floor base prevent you from scooping out the waste. My chickens' nighttime roosts are in the way when I clean, so I remove the screws that fasten them, take out the roosts, and re-install them after I have finished cleaning.

Lifespan of your Coop

If your coop is well-made of quality materials, it can last for many years. You can extend this by painting or staining the coop. Even if it already has a coat of paint, you might find it will need more coats. My chickens' coop is right below a large tree which drips water on it, so I had to do more than just paint the coop. I covered the whole top with roofing material, which has helped save the wood and cut down on leaks inside. Cheap hardware, like latches, tend to rust quickly also. Keep an eye on this and replace them as needed.

Visual Appeal

The coop needs to fit into your yard and life. For some people, the visual appeal is not a big deal, and this is especially true if no windows or neighbors look out on it. However, if your coop needs to be a focal point in your small yard, you may want it to look more like a gingerbread house than a converted shoe cabinet. There are many beautiful hand-crafted coops available as well as plans for making your own. By the same token, there are some pretty scrappy looking coops out there, too. At the end of the day, the final paint job can make even a moderate design look a good deal snazzier.

Transitioning Chickens to a New Coop

When I first got chickens, the chickens arrived in my backyard before I had finished building their coop. It was summertime, and relatively warm, so I placed some very nice perching sticks above their run area and covered the area with plywood for privacy. If you were a chicken, this would seem like a great place to spend a few summer nights until your coop was ready. Nearby, I placed an old bookshelf which I filled with straw that they could use as a nesting box to lay eggs in.

But they had their own ideas about this arrangement. The top shelf of the bookshelf was higher than the roosting perch and they noticed this. The chickens ignored the perch I built them and roosted on top of the bookshelf with their toes curled over the edge. They also ignored the "nesting box" on the shelf and instead laid eggs in the plastic pet carrier that they had arrived in (which I had left there after one chicken laid an egg in it thirty minutes after arriving). Despite my best efforts at planning, they had their own ideas about how to use the furniture.

When the coop was ready (complete with high roosts and nesting boxes), I put it on top of their run area, connected it with a ladder for easy access, and opened the windows so they would have enough light to see inside. But they refused to sleep in the new coop, continuing to roost on top of the bookshelf outside. When I took the bookshelf out of their area, they started sleeping on an outdoor roosting dowel on the top of the coop ladder. This is a good spot for sitting and resting during the daytime, but it is not even covered at night.

So I went to a fishing supply store, bought a small landing net, and caught each of my new chickens in the net one evening. I put them all in the coop and locked them in for the night, returning to let them out the next morning. After three nights of this, they became used to the coop, and started going inside every evening by themselves.

Some wooden dummy eggs in the nesting boxes helped them realize what these places were for. Since then, I have had other groups of chickens that also rejected the coop until I caught them and made them spend a couple of nights in there. Call it a hazing ritual for new chickens.

Chickens are predictable creatures for the most part, but they find small ways to be self-determined. For example, my current crop of hens will not use the three beautiful nesting boxes attached to their coop; they prefer to hollow out a nesting space in the straw on the floor of the coop (which is lined with straw bedding to catch their droppings). Because their nest is on the opposite side from where they sleep (away from the poopy side of the coop), I let them have their way and lay eggs there. Even though they have to stand in line and wait their turn to lay eggs in the floor nest each day, they have made it their spot.

Chapter 4: Feeders, Waterers, Nesting Boxes, and Roosts

In this chapter, we cover several required items. You will find out why they are important, where to get them, and how to place them in your coop or run space.

Feeders and Waterers

Chickens need to eat and drink. Feeding them can be as simple as scattering their food on the ground. But feeding and watering them every day is a chore and that is made far easier by placing more than a day's worth of provisions in their run area.

Any plastic or metal container can deliver either food or water. But bear in mind that it will be pushed, pulled, scratched, and landed upon, so a feeder either needs to be secured in place or it must be large enough that it won't tip over. You can put feeders and waterers indoors in a large coop, but they take a up a lot of space and make quite a mess with spilled food and water. I tried this for about three days and then moved them back outside.

Waterers are the most difficult to keep clean, because dirt gets kicked in them every day. I like to put both the feeder and waterer on top of cinderblocks, which cuts down on the quantity of material that gets kicked up there by chickens scratching on the ground. I also place them on opposite sides of the covered run area, so that no food gets into the water and wetness cannot spoil the food. Another idea is to hang them at an appropriate height. Assuming you have some high supports capable of holding some serious weight, this is a great way to gain a few more feet of ground space in the run area as well.

There are many types of poultry feeders and waterers you can buy, starting at less than $10. Some of the simpler waterers and feeders have some similar designs, so it is even possible to buy two of the same thing, filling one with food and the other with water. A good local farm supply or feed store will sell most of these types and they are available online as well.

The simplest option is a plain metal or plastic pan which you fill with water or feed. It may have a bracket on the back so you can prevent tip-overs by securing it to a fence, pole, or other part of your coop or run. Another design is a covered version of this pan with holes on different sides so different birds can eat or drink from it together. These feeders can be round or rectangular. The cover helps prevent birds from perching on top and fouling their food. This design is used frequently for chick feeders.

A larger feeder allows you to add more food at once and support more birds. A common design for these is a bucket feeder. You can even make one yourself. The basic concept is an overturned bucket on top of a wider dish. When the bucket is filled with feed, it spills out through holes at the bottom, onto the dish where the chickens can eat it. As the food on the dish is eaten, gravity sends more of it down through the holes.

The bucket-style feeder comes in several sizes with larger models able to hold up to 30 pounds at once. For perspective, a laying hen eats 4-5 ounces of food per day for about 8-9 pounds per month. This bucket feeder design also is used for waterers, most commonly from 3-5 gallons. Even though that is a lot of water, and it will last most small flocks for a few days, the water in the tray below usually gets pretty dirty within a couple of days.

These waterers need a swish or two every couple of days, which removes the dirty water as fresh water flows from the bucket to replace it. Fresh water is very important to chickens, which will stop laying pretty quickly when their water gets fouled. A few websites where you can see the different styles are www.randallburkey.com, www.strombergschickens.com, and www.mypetchicken.com.

The one kind of waterer that stays out of the dirt is a nipple waterer. This is commonly used in commercial chicken operations. Chickens touch the nipple to get a few drops from a hanging container and it never gets dirty or wastes water. I have tried these but cannot get my chickens to switch. Perhaps the change needs to be made when you get new chickens. The Avian Aqua Miser site sells these waterers as well as DIY kits to modify your own bucket with a nipple (http://www.avianaquamiser.com).

Automatic Waterers

There are several types of automatic waterers also, which are attached to a garden hose. These can either flow as a continuous fountain (which is more wasteful) or be controlled by means of a float switch like the one in your toilet tank. The latter design turns on the hose flow to fill the drinking dish and turns it off once the dish is full. I have seen a few of these online (at poultry supply sites like those listed above) and one local feed store sells a handmade version that looks like it should work just fine. You probably could make your own with a plastic container, float switch, hose fitting, and hose clamp.

Automatic Feeders

I now use what I consider to be an automatic feeder, which is the Chicken Tender Feeder. I bought it on eBay and it has been one of my best auction purchases. The Chicken Tender does not release food on a timer, though I have seen these for sale also. This feeder is closed to the outside world until a hen jumps on the feeder step, opening the feed door so she can eat her fill. I like this feeder because it holds 35 pounds in the hopper, which fills the eating area by gravity.

It also prevents any rodents from getting in because they are not heavy enough to open the door. Of course, the chickens still manage to spill some, so any rodent who got into the run probably could eat its fill, but it would not get into the main feed supply. Best of all, I no longer have to check the food supply daily or even weekly; this keeps them going for quite awhile. At the time of this writing, the following site (www.coopsnmore.com) was selling versions with capacities of 20, 35, and 70 pounds of feed.

Nesting Boxes

A nesting box is a cozy space where a hen can go and lay her eggs. Nesting boxes generally are closed on three sides for privacy and they can be filled with some bedding material like straw, sawdust, leaves, or shredded paper. The chickens will move this around until they have it how they want it. You also may want to consider lining the bottom of the nesting box with plastic because occasionally an egg will break and cause a mess. You *do not* want that rotten egg smell around, so the easier it is to clean a nesting box, the better.

Most coops come with 1-3 nesting boxes already installed, so you do not have to add anything. If you are building your own coop, this is one addition you can't forget. Usually, nesting boxes are attached to the coop wall with a door you can open from outside to harvest eggs, though the boxes also can be attached to a wall or fence. They should be raised off the ground with an easily accessible perch (such as a dowel or shelf) as a top step outside. Nesting boxes measure somewhere around 16-18 inches wide on each side and 20 inches tall. This is the perfect size for a laying hen.

Then again, you might build three beautiful nesting boxes like I did and have your hens prefer to lay their eggs on a floor nest of their own design. Hens also will nest in a five gallon plastic bucket that is left on its side and lined with a few inches of bedding material. Make sure it is wedged in or fixed to something so it doesn't roll around much. And preferably, it should be raised off the ground somewhere.

Roosts

As I mentioned earlier, chickens need some perches to sit and roost on. The most important furniture in your coop is a roosting bar or two. A one-inch thick dowel, branch, or stake placed across the inside of the coop is perfect. Make sure it is sanded enough so as not to create any splinters. It should be placed pretty high up, and it should sit right above where you want them to poop (certainly, away from the nesting boxes). After all, chickens do about half of their pooping at night so you will capture a lot of manure from the coop.

The base of the coop should be filled with carbon-rich bedding such as leaves, straw, sawdust, or shredded paper. Ideally, this catch area will be low enough below the roosting bar so that you do not have to clean it out more often than once a month or so. If the pile starts to stink before you scoop it out, throw another layer of bedding on top of the manure.

Chickens also appreciate having additional perches in the run area. They can rest on these during the day. Dowels, garden stakes, or branches about one-inch thick work very well.

Chapter 5: Getting Chicks or Chickens

You can obtain chickens at any phase of their early life: as fertile eggs, chicks or pullets (teenage chickens). If you buy fertile eggs, then you need to incubate and hatch them. You can also buy young chicks to raise or you can buy pullets that are ready to begin laying. For more information on chicken breeds, and which kind may be best for your needs, please see the "Learning About Chicken Breeds" section in the Resources section at the end of this booklet. There is also more information about the quietest chicken breeds in the "Quiet Kinds of Chickens" section of Chapter 9.

Raising chicks is a lot of fun and especially worthwhile if you have kids. But if you are a busy person with limited time for your new chicken hobby, or if you can't wait six months for eggs, I recommend you start with pullets. If you are getting just 3-4 hens, then buying pullets probably will save you money over raising chicks.

Raising chicks includes an up-front cost with the incubator and brooder equipment, which only pays for itself if you use it for a larger quantity of chicks. Also, consider the fact that it takes about 100 pounds of feed to raise one hen from the day she hatches until she starts to lay eggs. When you buy chickens as pullets, they can can live in the coop and be treated just like adult chickens, meaning that they are fairly independent. Most will begin laying eggs at 5-6 months of age.

Hatching Eggs

You can order fertile eggs online or obtain them locally from someone who breeds chickens. Often, you will see postings on Craigslist or in online poultry forums when someone has extra hatching eggs to sell. Occasionally, people even give away extra eggs. But it takes a great deal of care to harvest and care for hatching eggs, so most breeders are in it for a few well-deserved dollars. Also, there are not many roosters in urban areas (for good reason!), so fertile hatching eggs are pretty rare unless you drive out to the countryside.

The price of hatching eggs mostly depends upon the demand for a particular kind of chicken. For example, you can expect to pay more for French Copper Marans than for White Leghorn eggs. This is because the former is a rare variety that produces the darkest brown eggs of any chicken (they look like dark chocolate eggs and are prized by gourmet chefs). On the other hand, Leghorns are one of the most common commercial egg layers, producing most of the white eggs you see in supermarkets. Here is a picture of some Copper Marans eggs. This breed is covered as one of the exotics in my e-booklet entitled *Best Chicken Breeds*, which is available on Amazon.

The best selection of hatching eggs may well be found on eBay (www.ebay.com). I recently ran a search for "chicken hatching eggs" which returned over 400 results. I think you could find eggs for nearly any kind of breed on here. Of course, you are dealing with mostly amateur sellers, so you are never 100% sure what you are getting, but eBay sellers aim for quality to preserve their feedback and reputations.

To hatch eggs, you need an incubator. Incubators keep eggs warm at the same temperature (99.5 degrees) as a mother hen sitting on them. It takes about 21 days for the chicks to pop out of their shells. During this time, the eggs need to be turned three times a day, so that they stay universally warm rather than being cooked on one side and frozen on the other. Either you can turn them manually or you can buy an incubator that includes an automatic egg turner.

There are many different incubators on the market, but you can ignore the expensive ones built for commercial use. What you probably need is a small one that can keep 6-12 eggs warm at a time (however many you are hatching). All of the online hatcheries sell them and you can see some examples at these sites: www.strombergschickens.com, http://incubatorwarehouse.com, and http://www.brinsea.com. Many poultry supply sellers also offer incubator kits, which can include the incubator, a fan, an egg turner, an egg candler, and other accessories. A large kit may also include a brooder, which you otherwise have to buy or make yourself. Brooders are explained in the next section, which covers chicks.

Getting and Raising Chicks

You can order day old chicks from any of the hatcheries, which is their specialty. Chicks generally cost $1-$3 each, depending on the breed and quantity you order. The chicks are sent to you as fast as possible by U.S. mail, but try to find a hatchery in your region of the country to minimize transport time. When they hatch, chicks still have a three day supply of yolk in their bodies, so they do not need to eat during this time.

Most hatcheries have a minimum order size of 10 or 25 birds, since this body heat maintains an adequate temperature and humidity in the box. However, at least one hatchery offers a smaller minimum order size: try http://www.meyerhatchery.com or http://www.mypetchicken.com. Perhaps you can split a larger order with some other folks or else sell off the extra chicks (or pullets that you raise from chicks). Your local farm or feed stores may sell a few popular breeds of chicks as well. Ask them about the hatch date so you know how old the chicks are; they be a few days or a few weeks old.

To raise young chicks, you will need a brooder. The brooder is a warm place where the new chicks can stay for their first few weeks. The brooder has a heat source to keep chicks warm (usually a light bulb) and a box or container where they can stay during this time. Chicks need this extra warmth for their first three weeks or so. At 3-4 weeks of age, you can start transitioning the chicks into an outdoor coop and run by letting them spend a few warmer hours there until you move them permanently.

Brooder kits are sold by the same online suppliers who sell incubators (see above). If you would like to make your own, head to Google or Yahoo and try an online search for "brooder plans". Last time I looked on YouTube, there were a couple of instructive videos as well. If you make your own using a light, do not forget to put a thermometer in the brooder also so you can regulate temperature by moving the light in and out.

As a general guideline, keep the temperature in the brooder at 90-100 degrees for the first week and then decrease it by 5 degrees each week. The most effective method of setting the right temperature is to watch where the chicks gather. If they gravitate to the outside of the brooder area, the heat source is too hot. If they cluster near the exact center, it is too cold for them and they need more heat. Ideally, they will be somewhere in between, close to the heat source but not fighting each other for room at the exact center.

You will need a chick feeder and waterer also, which are easily obtained at a farm supply or feed store (see the previous section for more information on feeders and waterers, the smallest of which work fine for chicks). Feed young chicks with Starter Feed for the first 4-8 weeks (until they will eat pullet or adult feed, usually once they get some feathers). Always keep enough food and fresh water in the brooder.

You can line the brooder with cardboard or newspaper and cover this with a thin layer of bedding such as shredded paper, straw, or sawdust. Some people love pine or cedar shavings because of their fresh scent, while others claim that these aromas are toxic to young chicks. Aspen or hardwood shavings may be more reliable if you can get them. Be ready to scoop out and replace the bedding regularly as it gets dirty. Here is a shot of some chicks in a brooder box with a feeder.

Predictably, some chicks will be female while other will be male. Roosters have no place in urban yards, and are not needed for egg production. They are loud and obnoxious, offensive to neighbors, and banned by many local ordinances. Initially, all chicks will look about the same, and it is not until their combs and wattles start to fill out around 4-6 weeks that you will be completely sure about a young bird's gender. So you can try to sell the roosters or give them away. Hatcheries kill most of them, because most people want hens.

Hatcheries have three main ways of "sexing" day old chicks to determine their gender. First, there is a way that experts can squeeze the poop out of them (do not try it at home) to see if there is a bump inside that indicates the chick is male. Second, there is a difference with the feathers on some breeds that trained experts can detect.

Third, Red Stars, Black Stars, and any other so-called "sex link" chickens are bred so that males and females have different coloring right away. This is how hatcheries are able to sell you day old female chicks, male chicks, or "straight run" (as hatched) chicks, even though I just told you that normal people (you and I) cannot determine a chick's gender for several weeks.

Getting Pullets

Chickens begin to lay eggs at 5-6 months and enter the prime of their egg-laying abilities pretty quickly. Their first year of laying will be extremely productive, and their production rate will gradually decline after that. So if you are going to buy chickens, it makes the most sense to get them as pullets (young hens less than one year of age). Pullets are widely available and you probably can find some in your local area by checking classified ads (try www.craigslist.org) or asking if a local farm or feed store has pullets. Some hatcheries also sell them via online orders and can ship the pullets to your home, but you are better off finding some locally.

Pullets usually cost around $10-$25 per bird. When you think of the time and energy that goes into raising chicks, not to mention the cost of feeding each bird until it starts laying, buying pullets is a pretty good deal. Next time you are in the supermarket, see what they charge for the highest quality organic eggs, and realize you will be saving that much for every dozen that your hens lay (less the cost of any feed and supplies). Since I am busy working each day and keeping chickens is a very part-time hobby for me, I can tell you that buying pullets is my preferred, lazy person's method of obtaining chickens. Here is a picture of some pullets.

What to Do With Old Hens

This may be the most difficult question of all. After a year, laying hens start to decline in production. You may be satisfied with the number of eggs you still get for a second year…perhaps even a third year. But at some point, you must face the fact that your hens are eating the food but not producing at the same clip. Chickens live from 8-15 years and perhaps even longer. So at some point, you must decide to keep them as pets and start buying your eggs again, or else get rid of your aging hens.

Getting rid of the birds is tough to do, but it is a necessary step if you are serious about continuing to produce eggs from a small backyard flock. Also, it is tough to find anyone who wants your older hens. One strategy is to keep "dual-purpose" (good egg laying and good meat) breeds like Rhode Island Red, New Hampshire Red, and Barred Rock. You know what I have to say next: either you slaughter them yourself and turn them into dinner or else you give/sell them to someone else who will do this. I will not provide instructions on slaughtering a chicken, but I think you will find plenty of information about this online.

Keep this in mind: a lot of us treat our animals like cuddly pets and think of them that way. But on a farm, every creature has a purpose and usually turns into meat of some sort. Farmers need to make business decisions about animals, so there is a level of detachment to their decision-making that a lot of us cannot appreciate. As we have become more urbanized and moved further away from nature, we have forgotten where our food comes from.

Unless you are a strict vegetarian, you are paying someone else to raise and kill your meat. I am not telling you to slaughter your chickens for dinner, but I think it is healthier for us to get closer to our food sources. If this is what you decide to do, I will respect you for it. Just make sure that no city or county ordinance forbids animal slaughter…and that no neighbor sees you do it.

Another strategy is to sell or give away your chickens while they are still in their egg-producing prime. This method costs a bit more, because you are buying new chickens more often, but it is easier to get someone to take a 1.5 year-old ("18-month old") hen than a 3-year old. This is my preferred method of moving hens out, so I start asking around at about 1.5 years to see if there are any takers. We donated our last batch of egg layers to a local school, which was delighted at the number of eggs these hens were still laying.

As soon as the previous hens are gone, I start looking for new hens of the appropriate age and breed. This break gives me time to clean up the coop really well, perform any small repairs, and make sure that everything is predator and rodent-proof. Then I get some new pullets and start over. I wish I had a farm's worth of space and could keep a larger flock of younger and older hens, but in the space I have, this is the way I have to do it.

Chapter 6: Feeding Your Chickens

Take a drive through the American heartland, particularly the upper Midwestern states, and you will see miles upon miles of corn and soybeans. Corn and soybeans seem to be the easiest grain and protein crops to grow on an industrial scale, so they make the cheapest food for both people and animals. Commercial egg laying chickens are fed almost nothing but corn, soybeans, and a few vitamin and mineral supplements such as extra calcium for their eggshells. Unfortunately, this is not really a balanced diet, and it is very different from what chickens eat in nature.

Feeding your chickens well means beginning with a good quality feed. You can buy "chicken scratch" which is an assortment of cracked grains and seeds for them to snack on, but scratch grains do not provide them with full nutrition. For this, you need to buy a balanced chicken feed. Several companies make organic feed, which is available at farm supply stores and some pet stores in amounts ranging from five pounds to fifty pounds. Many such stores have bulk bins where you can buy the quantities you need of feed, scratch grains, and other supplements and treats. Here is a brief guide to the terminology used in chicken feed and when each type may be most appropriate.

Choose the Right Feed for the Age and Purpose of your Chickens

Starter Feed: This is finely ground food which is appropriate for chicks. Do not feed "adult" or "layer" feed to chicks, since it has a higher mineral content to support egg laying birds. Chicks should be fed starter food until they are 4-8 weeks of age; as soon as they will eat pullet food or adult food, you can start them on it. Chick feed is sometimes called "grower" feed, but this term is also used for pullet food, so make sure you know what you are buying.

Pullet or Grower Feed: From 4-8 weeks of age until hens start laying, some people feed them pullet rations while others just use an adult feed. Pullet feed is sometimes called "grower" feed, but since this term can be used for chick starter feed also, make sure you are buying the right food for your chickens' age.

Adult Feed: For fully grown chickens. This does not have additional nutrients to support egg laying. It is appropriate for older non-laying hens or for roosters (though roosters can eat layer feed too).

Medicated starter: Starter feed with a medication added to help prevent coccidia infections. This is the leading cause of death for chicks up until 16 weeks of age. It is picked up from feces, so the cleaner you can keep the chicks' water and living area, the better. Before using medicated starter, find out if your chicks have been vaccinated for this when hatched. Even then, many people choose not to medicate; coccidia naturally occurs in the gut of the chicken and they need to build up an immunity to it.

Broiler Feed or Broiler Rations: This is a formula of feed for birds that are being raised for meat. A more specific version is called "broiler finisher" for the last few weeks before they become dinner.

Size of the Feed

Pellets: The food is ground up and pressed into small pellets, which all look the same. Pellets are easy for most chickens to pick up, but chicks and small bantams should be fed a crumble or mash because pellets may be too big for them. The biggest advantage with pellets is that the chickens waste a lot less food than they do with the crumble or mash. Crumble and mash are mostly powder, and when this gets dropped on the ground, it is much less recoverable than pellets.

Also, it saves a little money if you can buy chicken feed in bulk quantities (such as 40 or 50 lb. bags). However, if you have only two or three hens, and particularly if you supplement their feed with kitchen scraps and whatever they can forage, then 40 or 50 lbs might last for six months. Crumble and mash tend to spoil in less time than that, with the oils going rancid, while the size and shape of pellets may preserve them a bit longer.

Crumble or Meal: This is ground-up food, which can appear as coarse as heavy cornmeal or as fine as powder. It's like the crumbs at the bottom of a box of crackers. Research has shown that hens lay most productively when fed in crumble form. However, the biggest downside is that they do spill a lot of it on the ground, which is difficult to recover.

Mash: Ground grains mixed with a nutrient batter. Add a little water of milk and it takes on a wet consistency like oatmeal. Chickens love this, probably more than any other form of food. Just like us, it is easier for their bodies to process wet food than dry food, though it gets all over their beaks and makes quite a mess. The downside is that the ingredients may be identifiable, giving chickens the ability to pick and choose, so a certain amount is wasted.

If you have a choice between different brands of chicken feed, ask to see the ingredient list for each one. Some will be made of corn, soybeans, and a few vitamin and mineral supplements. That provides little more than balanced protein; it does not provide much food diversity.

The kind of layer feed I normally buy is on the opposite extreme, but I think it is well worth a few more dollars. It includes all organic ingredients: corn, soybeans, ground flax seed, dried alfalfa, kelp meal, diatomaceous earth, garlic, juniper berries, and a few more ingredients. It is a whole food because chickens are not only getting their calories and protein; they are getting extra omega 3 fatty acids (from flax), another source of protein and greens (alfalfa), trace minerals (kelp meal), a natural de-wormer (diatomaceous earth), and more. For those opposed to soy, there are some soy-free blends on the market which usually substitute field peas as a source of legume protein (available online, if not locally).

There is nothing wrong with buying feed from large, national brands if those are the best feed sources in your area. I live in California, where Modesto Milling provides the high quality organic layer feed described above. Ask around at pet stores or farm stores in your area to see if there is a regional feed provider with a similar dedication to the chickens' diet. Even if your chicken feed contains mostly corn and soybeans, you can always supplement it by feeding your birds a few goodies. Before I discovered this feed, I used a plainer one, and just made sure to feed the hens plenty of fruits and veggies.

It is very important not to let chicken food get wet, moldy, or spoiled. You can keep it in the original bag, closing it up tightly and keeping it off the ground in a dry place. Alternatively, you can store the grain in a small garbage-type bucket or other storage container. Metal or heavy plastic containers can also discourage rodents, which are good at eating through bags.

Depending on heat and humidity, feed can spoil within weeks or it might last in a dry place over the winter for a few months. The biggest danger is that the oils can go rancid, which become toxic to chickens (and don't forget, you are eating their eggs). When in doubt, throw out or compost any old feed and get some new stuff.

Chickens also need two other supplements that you can buy at your local farm supply or pet store. First, they probably need extra calcium. Oyster shell is a great source of both calcium and trace minerals; you can buy oyster shell that is broken up into just the right pieces for the chickens to eat. Put some in a small feeder near their main food supply or scatter a small pile of oyster shell on the ground in their run. Alternatively, you can reuse their eggshells by washing them out well, microwaving them briefly to remove any pathogens, and breaking them up into small pieces. It might seem weird, but the chickens will eat the eggshells when they need more calcium.

Second, chickens need to eat some small rocks to break up hard grains. The small rocks you need are sold as "grit", which is non-soluble rock of just the right size, usually crumbled granite. This will not dissolve in the chickens' digestive system, providing them with the roughness they need to properly digest hard grains and seeds. Again, you could put some grit in a small feeder, mix it into the main food supply, or else just scatter a pile of it on the ground. Chickens will take what they need, which is somewhere around a ratio of 1/40 (grit/grains). If chickens are only eating commercial feed and no hard grains (such as scratch grains), then theoretically they do not need grit.

If your chickens are fortunate enough to range freely, even in a small yard, they will choose to eat a blend of food that is probably similar to what their wild chicken ancestors consumed. First of all, they will eat bugs, slugs, worms, and anything that crawls. If you are a gardener, this is great news, because your pest population will plummet as soon as you get some chickens. Bugs provide excellent protein for chickens and this immediately cuts down on the amount of feed you need to buy and feed them.

If your chickens do not have access to many bugs, they will need a little animal fat here and there. Some nutrients are only soluble through lipids, and feeding hens an entirely vegetarian diet is contrary to their nature. I give my chickens an occasional treat in this category and try to vary the source; one day it might be spoiled milk or old yogurt, while the next week it might be a few anchovies or a spoonful of cod liver oil in their scratch grain or a few anchovies.

Second, chickens love to eat greens. Young blades of grass are their first choice, and they can eat lots of grass each day. Health nuts will tell you that wheatgrass juice is great stuff to put in your body; a 2-ounce shot packs 70% of your daily allowance of vitamin A, 20% of your daily iron needs, a surprising amount of protein, plus loads of beneficial chlorophyll, enzymes, and minerals. You may not like to drink this stuff, but if your chickens want to eat lots of grass, think of how much more nutritious their eggs will be. Chickens also love to nosh on any other greens. Weeds like dandelion, dock, clover, wild mustard/radish, and chickweed are popular snacks.

Also, if you have a garden and grow lettuce, spinach, chard, kale, broccoli, or any other green vegetable, chickens will eat any leaves you would throw away. If you do not have a vegetable garden, feed them any old leaves of lettuce or spinach from your refrigerator. Wilted leaves or browned edges do not bother them. If you ask at the local grocery stores, the folks there usually will be glad to give away some old cabbage or chard that is past its selling prime. One way or another, get your chickens some greens and you will be amazed at how much they eat!

Third, chickens like fruit. If you have a fruit tree which drops some old fruit on the ground, chickens will clean up the area, leaving less for any neighborhood pests. I usually toss them any blemished fruit from our garden at harvest time. The rest of the year, our chickens get to pick through the trimmings of our fruit. Apple cores, melon seeds and peels, and overripe berries are all big hits with the cluckers. My family eats a lot of fruit, so the chickens get plenty throughout the year.

Chickens need their antioxidants too, so I always make sure to give them any overripe or blemished dark fruit that we have, such as blueberries, elderberries, plums, grapes, or cherries. You can ask about overripe fruit at the grocery store also. But be careful not feed your chickens anything with mold on it, which can make them sick just like us.

They are very attracted to orange-colored fruits and pumpkins, probably for the same vitamin A and beta carotene that provides our bodies with powerful sources of antioxidants. Melons, mangoes, papayas, apricots, winter squash and sweet potatoes are all chicken favorites. Studies have been conducted on chickens showing that these antioxidants can prevent infections of e. coli and other pathogenic organisms.

Even if you have a limited sized run area and your chickens only get a few bites of bugs and weeds, it will make a big difference. You can give them a more balanced diet by providing them with your kitchen food waste or compost. Chickens love to pick through your compost and peck at what they want, scratching and grinding the rest into the mulch or soil where it becomes great compost. By giving them your compost, you will save food from being thrown away and save money by having to buy less commercial feed for your chickens.

By now, you may be feeling sorry for those commercial egg laying chickens that eat corn and soybeans. They spend all their lives in confined indoor spaces and never even get a decent meal. As soon as you crack open your first home-raised egg, you will see the difference in these chickens' diets. The eggs at the store break easily and have pale lemon-yellow colored yolks.

Feed your chickens a balanced diet and their eggs will be healthier. The shells will be harder to crack from all that calcium, and the yolks inside will be nearly orange with beta carotene and other nutrients. Somewhere around 1/3 of the nutrition that a laying hen eats goes into her eggs, so eating home-raised eggs is like adding some spinach and salmon to your scramble.

The nutritional superiority of free range eggs has been documented in several studies. A few years ago, Mother Earth News (which is a great magazine by the way) ran a study that documented the differences. The study compared the U.S.D.A. nutritional content information for commercial eggs with the free range eggs produced from 14 different flocks in all parts of the

United States (as tested by a professional food laboratory). On average, these free range chicken eggs contained (compared with factory farmed eggs): 1/3 less cholesterol, 1/4 less saturated fat, 2/3 more vitamin A, twice as much omega-3 fatty acids, three times more vitamin E, and seven times more beta carotene.

Other studies have confirmed similar numbers. In 1974, the British Journal of Nutrition reported that pastured eggs also had 50 percent more folic acid and 70 percent more vitamin B12 than commercially produced eggs. More studies have found 3-4 times more omega-3 fatty acids in free range eggs. The typical American diet includes too much omega-6 in proportion to omega-3, and many experts blame this imbalanced ratio for high cholesterol and certain chronic diseases. Adding more omega-3 fatty acids to your diet may increase the levels of good (HDL) cholesterol in your body, while decreasing bad (LDL) cholesterol and overall cholesterol levels. Many people with high cholesterol avoid eating eggs, but maybe they should eat more home-raised eggs!

Chicken Treats

What kinds of treats do chickens like? Here is my Top Six list of snacks they gobble up in a hurry:

1. Melon seeds. The seeds from Cantaloupe, Honeydew, Galia, or Crenshaw melons are small enough for chickens to eat. They love pecking up these seeds along with the sweet, pithy material from the center of the melon. Whenever we eat melons, I scoop out the seeds and give them the peels to peck clean also. If you are cooking pumpkins or winter squash, they like these seeds and the stringy inside material also but you need to cut up the seeds first since they are larger. Putting them in a food processor for a few seconds reduces them to an edible size. These seeds are a natural de-wormer and provide healthy protein and oils for the chickens.

2. Small, dark-colored berries. Research studies have demonstrated that dark purple, dark blue, and dark red colored fruits are very high in antioxidants. Chickens need antioxidants to stay healthy, just like we do. I feed my chickens any overripe or spoiled (but not moldy) blueberries, elderberries, cherries, and grapes along with larger fruits in season like plums. They really love the berries and small fruits.

3. Seafood. You need to be very careful with leftover seafood. Obviously, feeding chickens something you found on a beach or in a dumpster involves a lot more risk of pathogens than sharing the leftovers from your refrigerator. Also, a lot of seafood contains high levels of mercury and other heavy metals, which are more concentrated in larger fish. That said, the chickens will quickly gobble up any seafood product from shrimp to anchovies to salmon; surely they must appreciate the protein, fat, and trace minerals. I had never thought of seafood as chicken food until I saw a picture of some jungle fowl (an ancestor of the domestic chicken) in their native environment in South Asia. The picture showed these birds on some rocks at a beach at low tide, picking at the mussels and shellfish. Chickens do love seafood!

4. Sunflower seeds. These are a staple in wild bird food and chickens love them also. The best kind for them, though, is not the large striped seed that comes from sunflowers in most home gardens. These are too large and hard-shelled for my chickens, though perhaps the largest breeds can handle them. A smaller type, called a black oil sunflower seed, is sold for bird treats in feed stores. Chickens love black oil seeds, which contain plenty of vitamin E and some key minerals. I give them more seeds in the wintertime, when they burn additional calories staying warm. If I mix black oil sunflower seeds with any other seeds and grains, the chickens never fail to eat these first.

5. Old milk or yogurt. Milk products contain calcium that laying hens need (to make eggshells), so this is one way to give it to your birds. Even sour milk, which is spoiled by a day or two, is a big treat for them, as is any yogurt, cottage cheese, or other dairy product. Chickens cannot handle too much fat, and this is a rich food that would be rare in their native environment, so moderate amounts are best. Also, milk will not provide them with enough protein, so this is a supplement only, not a substitute for their normal food. My chickens usually spill a lot of milk, so I have started mixing it with some whole grain flour or cornmeal first, letting this soak up the liquid first, and then giving them this paste to eat. It always disappears pretty quickly.

6. Soaked or sprouted grains. Like us, chickens assimilate wet food into their bodies better than dry food. Eating some dry grains and drinking water works fine for them, but a nice treat for chickens is to soak their grain in water or milk first and then let them eat it like a cereal. Sprouting grains is an even better idea.

To spout grains, cover the bottom of a bowl or jar with a few handfuls of grains like wheat, barley, rye, or oats. Soak the grains overnight, pour off the water, and then cover them with a wet paper towel. Rinse them once or twice the first day. As soon as you see a short sprout tail on most of the grains, rinse once more and then feed it to the chickens. Sprouted grains have more protein and less starch than dry seed grains, are rich in enzymes, and their nutrients are easier for the body to absorb. The last time I fed three hens some sprouted barley, they rewarded me with a dozen eggs over the next four days!

Hiding Their "Medicine"

Just like human kids, it is difficult to get chickens to eat some things we want them to eat. One example is flax seeds, which many feed stores sell. I think everyone probably knows that flax seeds are a great source of omega-3 in the human diet. Feeding flax seeds to chickens really boosts the healthy omegas in your eggs. There is only one problem: chickens will not eat flax seeds unless there is nothing else left to eat. This food is really low on their list of culinary preferences.

The only solution, if you are not fortunate enough to have a commercial feed that includes flax seeds, is to give them ground flaxseed meal and mix it into something they like to eat. Buying flaxseed meal is more expensive and you may have to get it in a human grocery store, but a little goes a long way. You can grind these seeds yourself, but they are very hard and sticky; you probably are better off buying the flaxseed meal instead. Mix it with a little milk and cornmeal, so they have to eat the whole mess, and they won't be able to avoid the flax.

Another supplement I have fed my chickens this way is kelp meal. I order small amounts of it online as a soil amendment for my garden. You cannot buy too much at once because it spoils quickly. Kelp meal is ground-up seaweed that provides an incredible array of minerals from the ocean, plus some healthy compounds from the plant itself. Again using the hidden food trick, I mix a couple of tablespoons of kelp meal into some old oatmeal, leftover beans, or something they like to eat.

Chapter 7: Tips for Cold Climates

Cold Climate Tips
If you live in a cold climate, you may have heard that many people overwinter chickens inside their coops. The chickens who lay the commercial eggs sold in supermarkets never see the light of day. I think it is a real mistake not to let your birds out. Even in a cold climate (I once lived in Wisconsin), the weather has to be unusually awful for chickens to want to stay in a coop rather than go outside. They will not freeze to death from going outside during the day. You just need to follow a few tips to help them get though the winter:

1. Make sure their water does not freeze by using a heated waterer. At least two kinds are available online, a standard waterer with a thermostatic heater inside a heated base for a metal waterer, which is good down to 10 degrees.

2. Give them all the food they need in wintertime (including some extra protein and fat), because they will not find as much food outside and they need extra calories.

3. If there is snow on the ground, cover it with a layer of soil, leaves, or other mulch so they can walk without freezing their feet.

4. Put some perches off the ground where they can sit during the day, again helping them keep their feet off the snow or wet soil.

5. For chickens with large combs and wattles, prevent frostbite by rubbing their wattles with a little petroleum jelly (like Vaseline) every few days. Breeds with shorter combs and wattles, which do not stick very far out, are less likely to get frostbite.

6. Insulate their coop. Sheets of Styrofoam, a few well-placed straw bales to block the wind, or some old moving blankets lining the walls will help take off the chill. Some people install a light bulb in the coop and keep it on, which can add a small amount of heat (just make sure it does not start a fire). A pet's heating mat is another option. Other chicken keepers insist the chickens can keep themselves warm, even in a cold climate, without any insulation or heating in the coop.

7. Some cold climate gardeners use a greenhouse as a run area in the wintertime. Any unused shed, carport, or garage space could be used also, but be prepared for them to foul it up. This only succeeds when you are able to cover the ground with deep mulch/bedding that can be removed for cleaning, such as straw, leaves, or sawdust.

Chapter 8: Health and Safety

It is no fun to lose a chicken. If you keep chickens for awhile, you probably will lose one sooner or later. The only thing worse than losing one is losing *all* your chickens to a predator that gets in the coop or to some infection that wipes them all out (though diseases on this scale are very rare). Fortunately, you can greatly reduce the risk of both problems by taking some simple precautions. This is not rocket science, and we have been over most of it already in this booklet, but I want to emphasize how important it is to protect the health and safety of your chickens.

Safety from Predators

Most predators hunt at night, when chickens are asleep in the coop. So preventing predator attacks should be as simple as having a well-made coop with no gaps or weak spots for predators to exploit. Depending on your location, possible predators may include raccoons, foxes, coyotes, bobcats, skunks, opossums, weasels, ferrets, and even rats. During the daytime, neighborhood dogs and hawks (especially with chicks) are probably the worst attack candidates.

For most urban chicken farmers, the most formidable foe you will face is a raccoon. Raccoons live in most parts of North America, they are big enough to kill and eat chickens, and they are smart enough to crack the locks on a Swiss bank vault (well, maybe not quite that crafty). Raccoons can separate flimsy panels, rip out poultry wire that isn't attached well, and open door hardware. But you should not have any raccoon problems if you build your coop out of strong materials and seal it shut either by locking the door or enclosing the coop in a run covered in poultry wire.

Raccoons, skunks, opossums, badgers, rats, and voles are all proficient diggers, though some are more determined than others. If you use poultry wire fences as a barrier, make sure to also line the bottom for at least a couple of inches on each side. As I wrote in an earlier section, rats were tunneling under my coop until I hammered in some heavy duty six-inch tall landscape edging all around the perimeter. I have not had any rodent signs since then. Rats can be classified as both pests and predators, because they have been known to attack sleeping chickens in the coop. More often, they just want the chickens' food, but you do not want them around either way.

To prevent nighttime predators, I have four more suggestions. First, feed the chickens any kitchen scraps or treats in the morning, so these will be long gone or buried deep in the mulch by evening. If you compost your wastes, use an enclosed compost bin or tumbler instead of an open pile. Food smells certainly seem to attract more critters at night.

Second, consider investing in a motion-activated light near the chicken coop. Some nighttime prowlers will be scared off when the light turns on. I have a solar-powered LED light near my coop and, since I installed it, I have noticed less signs of scratching in the soil around the coop (probably from skunks or opossums).

Lights do not seem to bother raccoons, but none have managed to break into my coop and they appear to have stopped trying after the first few failed attempts. Of course, raccoons still come around our place, and a couple of times have gotten into the compost, making quite a mess each time. Another attraction in dry weather is water; I awoke one night to strange sounds and found a raccoon dipping in one of our rain barrels. I have heard stories of them swimming in peoples' backyard pools. A former neighbor saw a raccoon climbing the window screen outside her kitchen; she turned the kitchen sink sprayer on it to shoe it away, but instead it stopped climbing and stayed there while she doused it. They really do like getting wet.

Third, tighten everything up in your coop (and run, if the coop is open to the run at night). Weasels and their kin can slip through very small spaces and kill all your chickens. And rats can get in just about any hole, though I think I have them beat with the half inch wire mesh. Cover any gaps, put in a few extra screws to tighten your defenses, and make sure the door locks require a high IQ to open.

Fourth and finally, cats can make short work of a rodent population. And owls prey on just about all of the predators mentioned above (at least, when they are juveniles). It may be hard to get an owl to take up residence, but you can get a good hunting cat. Cats do not tend to bother chickens. If you live in an area where bears or mountain lions are vexing your chickens, then you probably already know more than I do about defending against them.

Keeping Chickens Healthy

Despite the best planning and care, all animals get sick on occasion just like we do. Feeding chickens a balanced diet and keeping their area as clean as possible are probably the best ways to ensure their overall health. Below is a list of some common ailments for chicks and chickens. For a longer list of chicken diseases and treatments, including pictures to help you diagnose symptoms, Try the AvianWeb site and select the page on "Chicken Diseases" (http://www.avianweb.com). For serious illnesses, take your chickens to a veterinarian.

Chicks: Pasty Butt. If you are raising young chicks, watch out for pasty butt for the first few days. This condition causes their poop to stick to their bottoms. It can block them from being able to poop again, so this can kill them if left unchecked. All you need to do is wash their bottoms. Use a washcloth and some warm water to gently remove the poop and clean them up. Dry them off before returning them to the brooder.

Chicks: Coccidiosis. The Coccidia parasite naturally lives in the guts of chickens, but early in their lives, chicks have not built up an immunity to it. Coccidia can kill chicks. You will know they have it when their droppings become bloody, and they usually go downhill from there. Chicks pick up the parasite from feces, so the cleaner you keep their living area and water, the healthier they are likely to remain. Some hatcheries will offer to vaccinate day-old chicks for cocci (as well as another serious disease called Marek's). Anticoccidial drugs are available from veterinarians or you can feed your chicks medicated starter food, but most people choose to take the risk and lay off the extra medications. After the first 16 weeks, they should be out of this danger zone.

Chickens: Eggs Breaking Early. To make well-formed eggs, chickens need fresh water, a balanced diet, and plenty of calcium for the shells. Occasionally, an egg will break during laying or beforehand (the chickens usually will eat it, but you will need to clean up the rest or else face a terrible smell). Lack of calcium is the usual culprit for broken eggs. Give them more calcium by increasing the amount of oyster shell you feed them (or just put a few cupfuls of oyster shell in their run that they can peck up as needed). You can also wash old eggshells (from eggs you have eaten), put them in a bag, and smash them with a hammer until the pieces are about the same size as wheat grains. It may seem weird, but chickens will gladly eat their own eggshells again for calcium.

Chickens: Cropbound. Chickens have an organ called the crop inside the base of their necks near the breast. When they eat a lot of food, their bodies store some of it in the crop for later use. When a chicken has eaten a big meal, you can see this organ expand just below the neck. Occasionally, the food will be stuck in the crop and the chicken will stop eating. If this happens to one of your chickens, give it a few ounces of warm water with a tablespoon of olive oil. Hold the chicken and gently massage its crop area to get things moving again. This should cure all but the most serious cases, which require surgery.

Chickens: Mites and crawling insects can be reduced or eliminated by dusting the coop and nesting boxes with diatomaceous earth (DE). DE is a white powdery substance made from the fossilized bodies of small organisms. It is mined from ancient deposits and is entirely natural. DE poses no danger to people or chickens (unless you breathe enough to irritate your lungs). On the other hand, it kills bugs, whose exoskeletons are pierced by the sharp edges of the DE particles. The bugs then dry out and die.

Food-grade DE can be mixed into grain to keep any weevils or other bugs from becoming an issue. Dust the coop with it and mix a couple of cupfuls into your chickens' feed. Some DE proponents believe it also prevents intestinal parasites, though research studies so far have not demonstrated this. At the least, DE protects the grains and provides a little more calcium in a chicken's diet.

Again, for a longer list of chicken diseases and treatments (including pictures to help with diagnosis), the AvianWeb site (http://www.avianweb.com) should be helpful.

Chapter 9: Dealing with Neighbors, City Chicken Laws, and Other Urban Challenges

There are many reasons we choose to live in cities and suburban areas. Many of us need to be close to our jobs, our families, and various urban resources and amenities. Some of us feel most comfortable with an urban or suburban culture. There are many benefits, and some downsides, to living in densely populated areas. One trade-off, for backyard farmers, is that our activities are more restricted than they would be in the countryside. If you lived in the sticks, the nearest neighbor might be five acres or five miles away, while the local government would expect you to be using that land for agrarian activities like raising chickens and growing some of your own food.

Chicken Laws

Let's talk about chicken laws first. The good news is that most cities and local governments have laws which allow people to keep a limited number of backyard hens. The bad news is that there may be some additional restrictions.

Most chicken laws were designed either to protect public health, prevent animal cruelty, or both. The majority of them are overly restrictive, because they were written many years ago when people did not understand public health risks very well. With the more recent movement toward locally-produced foods, and the sharp increase in the number of people keeping backyard chickens, cities all around the United States and the developed world have been forced to reexamine (and in some cases, rewrite) their laws to permit people to keep a limited number of chickens for egg laying.

Normally, laws that restrict chicken keeping in your city or town are located in the city's municipal code, having been created by an ordinance enacted by a city council or board of aldermen. Whatever restrictions they have should be located in the public health or nuisance law sections of the code. You can read the city code on the city's website, ask for a copy of it at a local library, or go down to city hall and ask someone what restrictions they have on keeping chickens.

In unincorporated areas, the county governments may create some similar laws, though these tend to be more restrictive in the most densely populated areas. In general, there are six different kinds of restrictions. Some cities will only restrict one or two of these things, while others have chosen to make life more difficult. You can see an informal list of user-supplied chicken laws on the City Chicken website (http://thecitychicken.com, click on "Chicken Laws"), which also has other helpful resources for anyone getting started with chickens.

1.) **No roosters**. Many city ordinances ban roosters, which is fine, because hens can produce eggs without them. You don't need a rooster. They're beautiful birds, but are just too loud near neighbors.

2.) **Number of hens**. In some cities and towns, you are limited to keeping only two or three chickens in your yard, while others allow their residents to keep as many as 10 or 25 chickens. Still others cap the number pretty low, but allow for the possibility of additional chickens if a person obtains a permit. The permitting systems in many places are jobs programs, since the fees cover inspection costs, and this cycle self-perpetuates the need for more paperwork and bureaucratic hassles. But when it comes to chickens, some cities have smaller average lot sizes than others, and they may want to ensure that no one is trying to keep too many chickens in too small of a space.

3.) **Distance from neighbors**. These laws often specify that your coop or pen must be at least a certain distance away (e.g., 20, 40, or 50 feet) from any neighbor's residence. A few of them also state that your coop should be a certain distance away from your neighbor's fence or property line. I have seen a handful of examples allowing you to keep them closer with the neighbor's consent.

4.) **No slaughtering**. A few laws prohibit any animal slaughter within city limits. For most of us, this should not be a problem, since we keep chickens for egg production only. If you need to end the life of an old hen and turn it into dinner, then maybe you could drive it out of town for this scene of the movie. I suppose no one would be likely to notice you beheading a chicken at night or in your garage, etc. (but this is just a casual observation, since I am not encouraging you to break any laws).

5.) **Larger number of chicks**. I have only seen a few examples of this concept, which can allow you to keep a larger number of chicks (than hens) for a limited amount of time. Once the chicks reach a certain age (e.g., four weeks), they are treated as adult birds, so any restrictions on roosters or number of hens would kick in at that time. Presumably, you would sell or give away those that you do not need.

6.) **Sales restrictions**. A few cities have separate laws prohibiting the sale of homegrown produce within city limits. In California, both San Francisco and Oakland had such restrictions, but they were changed to accommodate community gardens and small urban farms. If you are planning to produce extra eggs and sell them, just take a close look at your local laws and make sure you would not be violating the letter of such a law (or that some stickler could not require you to get a sales permit before doing so).

Getting Your Law Changed

If your city's laws are too restrictive, get them changed. In San Carlos, California, there was a ban on backyard chickens until a fourth-grade girl convinced the city council to change the law. As part of a class project, she researched chicken laws in neighboring towns (all of which permitted some chickens) and lobbied city council members. In the end, she gained their unanimous approval for her proposal to allow people to keep up to four backyard hens. If a 9-10 year-old kid can get the law changed, so can you!

On the other hand, it is not always that easy. Some people trying to get laws changed have encountered stiff opposition. In 2007, a group of Chicago residents tried to get chickens *banned* in the city, though they failed with this and instead succeeded in inspiring an opposing group of chicken enthusiasts. Usually, opposition comes from a very small number of local residents, but these people can be quite vocal and well-organized.

In her book *City Chicks: Keeping Micro-Flocks of Laying Hens as Garden Helpers, Compost Makers, Bio-recyclers and Local Food Suppliers* (Good Earth Publications 2010), Patricia Foreman documents the steps she took to get her local laws changed in Lexington, Virginia. The book includes copies of letters written, including those written by one local resident who opposed having chickens in the city. If you conduct a video search on YouTube (for "chicken laws" or something similar), you will see that others have posted accounts of their experiences also.

In this age of social media, blogs, instant messaging, and instant videos, it is becoming much easier to share your story with others. This, in turn, can allow a few committed people to quickly mobilize other like-minded citizens to sign a petition, send an e-mail, or attend a city council meeting. As more city residents have turned to keeping backyard chickens in recent years, a lot more people have gained familiarity with this pursuit as friends, family members, or neighbors of chicken-keepers. This has blunted opposition even more, because people have realized that hens are pretty quiet and have no noticeable impact on the noise, smells, or flies in an area.

In order to make a good argument to change the law, you need to do four things. First, create a list of some solid arguments in support of your position. What are some good reasons for a city to allow chickens? The first two paragraphs of this booklet contain several reasons to keep chickens, but by writing them out yourself, you will learn, understand, and believe in these arguments. Second, make a list of possible arguments the opposition might make (e.g., noise, smells, flies, public health, etc.). Roosters are noisy, hens are not, and especially many modern breeds are extremely quiet to the point where a neighbor will not even know they are there.

Smells and flies are barely existent when you use lots of bedding or mulch (leaves, straw, sawdust, or shredded paper) to cover the chicken poop. With public health, some people are worried about avian flu, but this disease has so far been largely restricted to people who work in large poultry operations in Southeast Asia and a few other places. If such a disease were to spread, an outbreak would be far more likely to take off in the factory-farmed chicken operations than in small backyard flocks. And you can continue yourself with the opposition arguments.

Third, to change the law, you need to be able to show how the current law is deficient and inadequate in meeting your needs. Here, it helps to have your mobilized group of neighbors and friends rally around you and present the common voice of the community in support of your position. Fourth, be ready to explain how the law should be changed. Conducting some research into other cities' laws is helpful, particularly those in the region where you live.

Your city board or council wants to keep up with the Joneses, and they do not want to be the only ones handling the chicken restriction in an archaic fashion when their local competitor towns have all joined the modern bandwagon. Print out copies of laws you like in other local cities and towns; present these to your local lawmakers so that they can have a blueprint for how to re-write the law in your town. Or, draft a new sample law yourself and present it to them, along with a petition full of signatures or a bag full of letters supporting you!

Lastly, I will mention that there are cities and towns with restrictive chicken-keeping ordinances that never enforce them. People in my area are supposed to trim their hedges at a certain height also, and no one ever does. City codes present someone's ideal vision of neighborhood planning and, unless an overzealous city inspector comes by or unless a neighbor calls you on something, you may be able to do things your way and have no trouble for many years.

On the other hand, would you spend extra money to invest in a larger coop if you knew the city could require you to keep fewer chickens? If you depend on a few bucks a month from selling extra eggs, what if someone were to take this away by pointing out that the law only lets you keep half that many chickens? Laws provide stability and predictability, which we sacrifice when we violate them. So if it is important to you to live within the law, get that law changed to accommodate your life.

Neighbors

Most neighbors are great and they love fresh eggs! Yet some neighbors can present the same kind of obstacles to chickens as a city, only on a smaller and closer scale. Most of them have never been around chickens, so they may have unfounded objections related to noise, smells, flies, or disease. These objections are based on mistaken assumptions, not reality. As mentioned above in the section on chicken laws, you can counter these objections with solid facts.

However, logic cannot convince some people, who would prefer to dwell in their own universe of misunderstanding and misinformation. This is where psychology and human relations come in. You need to treat them with respect, listen to what they have to say, and slowly try to change their minds while also being ready to help them. How can you help them? Be being willing to compromise a little if this helps (e.g., start with fewer chickens, agree to build a taller fence, or try a three-month trial period and see how it goes). What you do not want to do is force the neighbor to an opposing side.

Imagine that there are two TV channels available in your area. You are watching the "reality" channel while your neighbor is stuck on the "seriously whacked out" channel. But do not criticize that person for mistaken beliefs or perspectives, because it will be counter-productive. If you need that point proven, I have a terrible relationship with one of my neighbors as a classic example of me messing this up.

What you need to do is talk to them on their level, knowing that they are watching the "seriously whacked out" channel. Don't accuse them of this, but help them to slowly turn their channel to the "reality" network. It takes time, patience in listening to their dumb ideas, and giving them some free eggs, to get that channel fully changed (or at least changed on the chicken issue, since they may still be whacked out about everything else!).

If your local laws allow you to keep chickens, and if you are complying with the laws, then at the end of the day, your neighbors have very little power. One source of power for them might be a local noise ordinance, which often sets a maximum level of noise that may occur. If your chickens are too loud, then this is something you should address with them anyway, but a local noise law could allow them to bring in the police or city enforcement officials to cause you more trouble.

In general, this is extremely unlikely. Most hens do not make that much noise. Roosters are the ones who crow (some crow at all hours, not just in the morning). Hens will crow when an egg is ready, and sometimes one will crow to 'protect' another hen who is laying (this is known as "cheerleading"), but most of them just cluck at low volumes. The hens who crow most tend to be the younger ones, and oftentimes this behavior disappears after a few months.

If you are following the law, then you have as much right to keep chickens as you do to keep dogs. Remember that, and deal with any objections with the same confidence as you would bring to a discussion about your dogs. Almost every neighbor around me has dogs and all of them are louder at some point in the day than my chickens (a fact which I would point out if anyone ever called the authorities on me).

Also, chickens are quite silent at night when people really need quiet. My chickens wake up around seven o'clock most days and eat before they lay, so if there is any laying noise, it usually happens later in the morning between about eight o'clock and noon. By that time, even on our "quiet" residential street, there are dogs, crows, leaf blowers, garbage trucks, and all manner of other ambient noise, and many neighbors are gone for the day already.

If I am home when I hear crowing, I will go out there and feed the loud bird some treats to keep her busy while her friend finishes laying. I also have tried the Pavlovian opposite of turning on a sprinkler hose, but that only made the poor bird more nervous. Unless your coop is very close to your neighbor's residence or unless you get the luck of the draw with an unusually loud hen, you should be fine. And if there is no local noise law, your neighbor may just have to buy some earplugs to wear for 15 minutes in the mid-morning.

Before getting hens, I researched the topic of which chicken breeds are quietest. The consensus seems to be that some breeds tend to be quieter than others, but it is always possible to get the luck of the draw. Chickens are individuals and they each bring their own unique personalities. If you end up with that one loud hen, you may want to return it and exchange it for another. Based on my review of online forum postings about which chicken breeds are quietest (which is very anecdotal), the breeds mentioned most often as quiet were Ameracaunas (Easter Eggers), Australorps, Brahmas, Cochins, Delawares, and Red Stars.

For a more detailed overview of the best chicken breeds for backyards, please see my e-booklet entitled *Best Chicken Breeds*, which is available on Amazon.

One Last Thing: Dealing with Other Obstacles

I'd like to end this booklet by making one last point. As you journey into the world of raising chickens, you may encounter other urban obstacles, in which case you should consult others who may have faced similar issues. One great set of resources is the online forum sites mentioned in the Resources section at the end of this book, where many dedicated people volunteer their time to provide fellow users with important information. Also, ask around locally or un an online search to see if there is a group of poultry enthusiasts or backyard chicken keepers. Your local Master Gardner program, pet store, or veterinarian's office may be able to refer you to a local organization. There is nothing like having a mutual support network, whether it is local or online.

One challenge you will encounter in a small city yard is what to do with chicken waste (essentially, bedding material with manure in it). I sincerely hope you compost it, which is as simple as shoveling this waste material into a compost bin or tumbler, then letting it compost. There are many small bins and tumblers available for city dwellers, providing you with a way of recycling nutrients that is hygienic, rodent-proof, and nearly odor-free. Your local government may subsidize compost bins or worm bins for local residents, or else you can check online for some possibilities. Chicken manure compost works like magic on your garden. Since most of my writings are about fruit and vegetable gardening, you are welcome to browse my "Other Publications" section below if you would like to read more in that field.

Finally, another obstacle we encountered was homeowner's insurance. We obtained a low rate from an insurer who later dropped us from coverage by way of a letter. In the letter, the company stated that our policy was being dropped because there are "chickens on the property, which makes the risk unacceptable." Never mind that the previous week, in the next town over, a woman had been mauled to death by her own pit-bull. Dogs are OK, but just imagine the damage and havoc that a couple of five pound egg-laying hens could unleash! If it doesn't fit in their actuarial formulas, they can't handle it.

Under most states' laws, if this happens to you, the insurer must give you a reasonable notice period to find another carrier before you are dropped. We got a quote from a different company with the same rate which never asked about chickens in their application. A few months later, we received a strange notice in the mail from the new company stating that their property inspection had revealed we had a *barn* on our property, and it asked us to inform them whether we had any saddle animals. We replied that we have no saddle animals, and since then we have not heard from them again. I am still not sure what kind of saddle animal would fit in a chicken coop the size of a large bathtub!

I wish you the best of success raising chickens. I think you will find it is lots of fun, very productive in terms of fresh eggs, and much less work than taking care of other pets (who often just eat and sleep!). Please utilize the resources in the next section to obtain anything you need online or find support for any issues that arise. Cluck cluck!

Resources

Learning About Chicken Breeds

The best resource is my e-booklet, *Best Chicken Breeds: 12 Types of Hens that Lay Lots of Eggs, Make Good Pets, and Fit in Small Yards (Plus Bonus: 5 Varieties of Exotic Poultry)*. This e-book download is available on Amazon.

Here are some other great resources on chicken breeds:

1. Henderson's Handy-Dandy Chicken Chart at Ithaca College provides an in-depth overview of more than 50 types of chickens. Presented alphabetically, the chart explains breed coloring, weight, and origins as well as egg color and productivity along with notes on brooding and behavior. For example, it will tell you that Naked Neck Turken Chickens were developed in Transylvania before 1700, they lay creamy white eggs with good productivity, and they tend to

be adaptable to confinement and easily handled. These are just the kinds of things an urban chicken keeper needs to know. http://www.ithaca.edu/staff/jhenderson/chooks/chooks.html

2. My Pet Chicken's Chicken Breeds list. Shows you pictures of each kind of chicken and lets you compare breeds on one page by egg color, productivity, and cold hardiness. This site also has a Breed Selection Tool, which allows you to specify which qualities are most important to you (such as cold hardiness or docile nature) and it returns you the top choices based on the criteria you set. To use this selector, click on "Breed Selection Tool" in the Free Tools menu on the left side of the page. http://www.mypetchicken.com/chicken-breeds/breed-list.aspx

3. The magazine Mother Earth News surveyed its readers about the best backyard chicken breeds based on several factors. Their top choices were Rhode Island Whites (not Reds), Plymouth Rocks, Orpingtons, Australorps, and New Hampshires. I should add that the readers of this magazine tend to prefer heritage and heirloom varieties of all things and that most of them live in rural areas. So if there is a modern mixed breed that has some attributes important to city folks (relatively quiet nature and able to handle some confinement, such as an Easter Egger or Red Star), it might not make this list. Here is the article, which otherwise is excellent. http://www.motherearthnews.com/Sustainable-Farming/Best-Chicken-Breeds-For-Backyard-Flocks.aspx

Getting Chickens

1. Local Pullets. If you are buying pullets (young hens almost ready to lay), then it is best to look locally first. Try your regional Craigslist site, and look under the "For Sale" category for the "Farm+Garden" link and local classified ads. You can try a key word search for "chickens" or "hens" or "pullets" or "chicks" too. Alternatively, ask at your local farm supply or feed store, which may sell chickens or know who else does. Or you can post your own ad on here explaining what you are looking for, using a blind e-mail address. You never quite know what you are getting from a classified site, but most people (though not all) are honest and good. www.craigslist.org

2. Buy/Sell/Trade/Free. Some online poultry forums have organized threads for sales and barter. One good one is Chicken Chatter, which has a forum called Buy/Sell/Trade/Free. Last time I looked on there, one poster was selling hatching eggs for several varieties for $8-24, depending on the breed, while someone else was trying to find some French Copper Marans chicks (Copper Marans are famous for laying the most beautiful dark chocolate-colored eggs with a tint of copper). http://www.chickenchatter.org

3. Hatchery Chicks or Eggs. Try to find one in your area of the country, please, as chicks or eggs are shipped to you by mail or other carrier. Most hatcheries have order size minimums. Examples are McMurray Hatchery in Iowa, http://www.mcmurrayhatchery.com , Mt. Healthy Hatchery in Ohio http://www.mthealthy.com/ , and Ideal Poultry in Texas http://www.ideal-poultry.com/ . I do not have experience ordering from hatcheries and therefore I cannot endorse any of these places. Here is a directory of many more, sorted by online popularity. http://www.top20sites.com/Top-Poultry-Hatcheries-Sites

4. Egg Farms. I once came across an online posting where someone reported that he/she had obtained some laying hens from a local egg farm. This was a local free range farm, not a cruel egg factory. After a certain point, these folks may not want to keep the chickens anymore, even if they are barely past egg laying prime and still have a year or two of decent production left. Local egg farms often sell at farmers markets; ask if they have any extra hens to give away.

Chicken Coops and Supplies

1. DIY Coop Designs to Build Yourself. Do not pay for Coop Plans. The Backyard Chickens site has literally thousands of user-submitted designs, complete with pictures, materials lists, and schematic plans. What a wonderful resource! Go to the site and click on "Coops". http://www.backyardchickens.com

2. Local Builders. Try an online Google or Yahoo search specific to your location (for example, "chicken coop seattle"). You should find some local builders. Ordering a ready-made coop from very far away incurs some huge shipping costs (often more costly than the coop itself), so local is best if you can pick up the coop or have it delivered in your area. A general "chicken coops"-type search will yield some interesting results, too. Of course, these vary greatly in quality and price.

3. Local Classified Ads. Check out the classified ads on your regional Craigslist. Beware that some people have been ripped off by "sellers" on this site, so it is best to meet the person and see an example coop before you send money to a stranger. But it offers the possibility of finding a good local craftsperson who can make you an affordable coop…or someone giving away a used version. www.craigslist.org

4. Your Local Pet Store, Feed Store, or Hardware store may stock some coop models. They are likely to be the mass-marketed pre-fabricated coops made from the cheapest possible materials. These are not as strong as hand-crafted versions, but can get you started adequately. Just be aware that you may need to replace the latch when it breaks, add another coat of wood stain to get it through the winter, put in few more screws to strengthen the coop against predators, and that sort of thing. Here is an example of one line of pre-fab coops: http://www.waremfginc.com.

5. eBay. When in doubt, see what's on eBay. You never know what you'll find. www.ebay.com

Excellent Books for Deeper Knowledge about Raising Chickens

1. *Storey's Guide to Raising Chickens* by Gail Damerow (Storey Publishing 2010). This is the only in-depth book on chickens you will ever need. It is simple to follow, comprehensive, and an excellent resource for all. The author has written several other books on chickens and larger livestock.

2. *Raising Chickens for Dummies* by Kimberley Willis and Rob Ludlow (For Dummies 2009). I know you're not a dummy. Written by two knowledgeable people, this is a concise, no nonsense overview of everything you really need to know.

3. *City Chicks: Keeping Micro-Flocks of Laying Hens as Garden Helpers, Compost Makers, Bio-recyclers and Local Food Suppliers* by Patricia Foreman (Good Earth Publications 2010). This wonderful book provides a healthy perspective on the synergies between gardening and keeping chickens. As a backyard chicken keeper and gardening author, I thought I knew a few things, but I learned a great deal from reading this book.

Getting Your Questions Answered

1. The Backyard Chickens site has a great Internet forum for chicken lovers. As with the other forums below, this is largely a caring community of folks who are happy to share their wisdom and expertise. You can search through many thousands of posts using keywords to answer your questions, or you can pose a new question in the forums. For example, you might have a question like "I want to get chickens, but the coop would be right behind my neighbor's house. Which kinds of chickens are quietest?" Try a keyword search of the forums for "quietest chickens" and you will be well rewarded. This site sells coops and supplies, too.
http://www.backyardchickens.com/

2. PoultryOne is another helpful forum for getting questions answered. This is organized into several specific forums. There is a general chicken raising forum on the site called "The Chicken Coop" as well as more specialized choices like "The Incubator" (with chick hatching discussions) and "The Chicken Hospital" where problems caused by predators and diseases are covered.
http://poultrycommunity.com

3. The Poultry Keeper site has a good forum, too. It is based in Britain. They have a particularly active poultry trading thread, which I got excited about until I realized the prices were in pounds sterling and the members trading eggs were 5,000 miles away. Great information on here for everyone, though.
http://forums.thepoultrykeeper.co.uk/index.php

My Other Publications
(All are available on Amazon.com)

1. *Best Chicken Breeds: 12 Types of Hens that Lay Lots of Eggs, Make Good Pets, and Fit in Small Yards (Plus Bonus: 5 Varieties of Exotic Poultry)*

Overview of the best chicken breeds for backyards, including full color pictures of each type. Learn which types of hens lay the most eggs, have friendly and calm personalities, and fit well in small city back yards.

Topics Include:

• How This Information Can Help You
• Rainbow Eggs: White, Blue, Green, Dark Chocolate Brown, and More
• Importance of Hatching Eggs and Handling Chicks Early
• Each Chicken is an Individual

• Best Breeds: 12 types of hens that lay lots of eggs, have friendly and calm temperaments, and fit in city backyards
• Bonus: 5 Exotic Poultry Chicken Breeds for backyards: wait 'till you see these!
• Resources Section: Links to additional information on chicken breeds, plus where to obtain your chickens

Thinking about getting chickens? Not sure what kind is best? If you're ready to learn which types of hens lay lots of eggs on a regular basis, make good pets, and fit happily in small sized yards, you've come to the right place. This e-booklet, which is a companion to R.J. Ruppenthal's Backyard Chickens for Beginners: Getting the Best Chickens, Choosing Coops, Feeding and Care, and Beating City Chicken Laws, provides you with information on 12 types of chickens which are best suited for a small back yard flock. Also included is a bonus chapter covering 5 Exotic Poultry Chicken Breeds which are also suitable for backyards. If you've never seen a bird that looks like a chicken crossed with a turkey, another one with a head resembling a feather duster, a third that looks more like a rabbit than a chicken, a hen that lays dark chocolate brown eggs, and a one pound chicken 6-12 inches tall that people keep as an indoor pet, then prepare to meet some new friends! Amazingly, each of these has a friendly personality and all can make good pets.

There's a lot of free information online about different kinds of chickens. It's great to have this available, but sorting through it can take a lot of time. When I decided to get chickens, I spent many hours researching different chicken breeds in books and on the Internet. At the time, I had a small yard in the city. The only thing I knew about chickens was that the hens lay the eggs and the roosters make most of the noise!

From my research, I learned that there are as many as 175 different kinds of chickens in the world. However, only 12 chicken breeds met my criteria, which were:

• Regular and prolific egg layers
• Comfortable in an enclosed coop and run area
• Preferably, not too loud
• Friendly around people

It would take you at least two or three hours just to find this information, even before you sort through, read, and analyze it. You can find it all in this short e-booklet, which makes a great supplement to this book.

2. *How to Grow Potatoes: Planting and Harvesting Organic Food From Your Patio, Rooftop, Balcony, or Backyard Garden*

Perfect beginners guide to growing potatoes. This booklet explains how to plant and grow organic potatoes for food in the home garden. Recommended for backyard gardeners and container gardeners with small city-sized yards, patios, balconies, decks, and rooftops.

• Why Grow Potatoes? Six Great Reasons
• Different Kinds of Potatoes (and Where to Get Them)
• Growing in Containers, Raised Beds, and Traditional Rows

- Planting and Hilling Potatoes
- Soil, Fertilizer, and Watering Needs
- Harvesting Potatoes
- Storing Potatoes for Later Use
- *Bonus*: Two Secret Tips for Getting More (and More Delicious) Potatoes

3. *Blueberries in Your Backyard: How to Grow America's Hottest Antioxidant Fruit for Food, Health, and Extra Money*

Description from Amazon:
Perfect blueberry growing guide for beginners. This booklet explains how to plant and grow blueberries in the home garden. Recommended for backyard gardeners with small city-sized yards, patios, balconies, decks, and rooftops. (Updated 2012 version)

Topics include:
- Why Grow Blueberries? Six Great Reasons
- Blueberries for Every Climate (and where to get them)
- Grow Blueberries Almost Anywhere: Doorsteps, Patios, Balconies, Rooftops, and Yards
- Perfect Blueberry Soil (regular garden soil kills them, but they will thrive in this!)
- How to Plant and Grow Blueberries in Raised Beds and Containers
- Feeding, Watering, and Caring for Your Blueberry Bushes
- Making Extra Money Growing Blueberries

4. *Fresh Food From Small Spaces: The Square-Inch Gardener's Guide to Year-Round Growing, Fermenting, and Sprouting*

This book covers small space gardening, fermenting (yogurt, kefir, sauerkraut, and kimchi), sprouting, plus chickens for eggs and bees for honey. Over 20,000 people have read this book, which helps beginners learn what they can grow in small urban spaces, such as apartments, condominiums, townhouses, and small homes. Many readers have been motivated to try new things and grow some food where they did not believe they could before reading this. The book is a broad overview, so it does not have a fine level of detail.

Author Info

R.J. Ruppenthal is a licensed attorney and college professor in California who has a passion for growing and raising some of his own food. He regularly writes and blogs about fruit and vegetable gardening, growing food in small urban spaces, sustainability, and raising backyard chickens. On occasion, he even puts his degrees to use and writes something about law or government. You can follow his blogs at http://backyardcvf.blogspot.com or on his Amazon Author's Page.

Photo credits:
Chicken Tractor: Flickr user "Will Merydith", www.flickr.com
Chicks: Flickr user "goosegrease", www.flickr.com